King's Col
Cambridge
a personal view

King's College Cambridge, a personal view

ALAN MACFARLANE
with
PATRICIA MCGUIRE &
BRIDGET STREVENS
MARZO

CAM RIVERS
PUBLISHING

2018

First published in Great Britain
by Cam Rivers Publishing Ltd
2018

5 Canterbury Close
Cambridge CB4 3QQ

Devised by Zilan Wang
Written by Alan Macfarlane
Illustrated by Bridget Strevens Marzo
Supported by Patricia McGuire
Typesetting and layout design by Jaimie Norman
Marketing Manager James O'Sullivan

Printed and Bound in Great Britain.

ISBN 978-1-912603-27-5

www.cambridgerivers.com
press@cambridgerivers.com

Contents

Maps quick reference

Before your tour

You ARE ALLOWED to walk round and enjoy this ancient and unique College. We hope it is a marvellous experience for all of you.

Please remember, however, that the College is primarily a place of education, religion and research, where students and staff live and work. It is a private space, opened to the public at certain times and under certain conditions.

Please behave as if you were going into someone's private home, which is what the College is. Do not play music, drop litter etc. The most important thing is that you show respect and care as you move around.

Please look carefully at all the signs which tell you where you can go, what you can film and photograph. Please do not go into private doors and courts which are not open to the public. And please follow the instructions and advice of the staff of the College (porters, visitor assistants) if they approach you.

Some places mentioned in this guide are not open to the general public. They are indicated by a no entry sign on the map inside the back cover.

The number of visitors to King's is increasing rapidly because of the fame and beauty of the College. Please behave with extra care so that future visitors will continue to be able to come and enjoy the College.

※※※

This booklet has been written by Alan Macfarlane, a Fellow of the College for over forty years and currently a Life Fellow and Emeritus Professor of Anthropology. It is written in collaboration with PatriciaMcGuire, the King's College Archivist, illustrated by Bridget Strevens Marzo who studied at King's, and assisted by the Fellow Librarian Peter Jones.

The tour

WHEN YOU VISIT King's College on a beautiful summer's day, or when the snow covers the antique roofs, you are almost bound to be charmed and perhaps entranced. The place feels as if it is magical. King's has the charm of a place which is not quite real. It is light, open, inviting, and yet constantly elusive. The day visitor may sense that there are depths and riches, stores of buried knowledge and experience, a thick web of stories and legends here. Yet these are only glimpsed, shadows disappearing around a corner or along a sunbeam. Where does this special effect lie?

We are attracted to places which allow our minds and imaginations to expand. Many visitors know that King's is old – but is it *all* old, and how old is it? Parts feel very ancient, but beside them are obviously modern features. What we experience in this College leads the mind out of the present, across the bridge of the twentieth and nineteenth centuries with its industrial revolutions, back through to the classical forms of the Enlightenment, and then further back into the middle ages. To walk into King's is to enter a time machine, but one which needs some explanation for it is only partly visible on the surface.

The close juxtaposition of contrasted architecture in King's can be comfortably absorbed because there are wide gaps, lawns, trees and courts which separate the buildings. So you can stroll through a checkerboard of English history, see its styles and periods laid out in a calm, irregular yet controlled, fashion.

As you walk you will sense that the ideas of each of the periods over the last six centuries are not only to be found embalmed in stone, wood and glass. They survive inside these buildings in styles of philosophy, poetry, music, mathematics or theology which are still alive.

It is a College full of surprises even for those who have been in the College for some decades. Every day we discover new things which we had not known or noticed. We hope that this little guide will help you to share in the excitement of these discoveries.

Before you enter the College

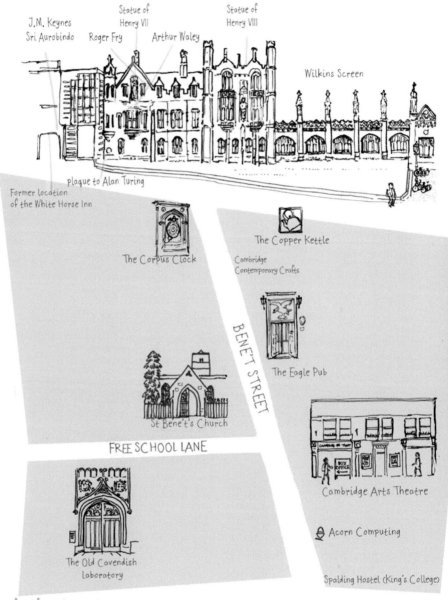

J.M. Keynes
Sri Aurobindo   Roger Fry

Statue of
Henry VII   Arthur Waley

Statue of
Henry VIII

Wilkins Screen

plaque to Alan Turing

Former location
of the White Horse Inn

The Corpus Clock

The Copper Kettle

Cambridge
Contemporary Crafts

BENE'T STREET

The Eagle Pub

St Bene't's Church

FREE SCHOOL LANE

Cambridge Arts Theatre

Acorn Computing

The Old Cavendish
Laboratory

Spalding Hostel (King's College)

from left to right, top to bottom:
Sri Aurobindo, Indian mystic and philospher
J.M. Keynes's rooms were in a previous buiding here
and also at 17A St Edward's Passage (lower right)
Former location of the White Horse Inn, 'little Germany'
Plaque to Alan Turing, computer scientist and cryptographer
Roger Fry, artist & English promoter of post-Impressionist and Chinese art
Arthur Waley, translator of the classics of Chinese and Japanese literature
Statue of Henry VIII installed in 1880

King's Porters Lodge

Chapel

Horse chestnut tree

cobbles

KING'S PARADE

King's College Visitor's Centre

ST EDWARD'S PASSAGE

17A St Edward's Passage above David's bookshop

St Edward's church

Market Hostel (King's College)

Wilkins Screen, designed by the architect William Wilkins and built in the 1820s
cobbles in front of the Porters Lodge
Horse chestnut tree, a focal point of the University
The Eagle Pub where the discovery of DNA was announced
Old Cavendish university laboratories - DNA, electrons, neutrons
Acorn Computers, pioneering computing started here

King's College ('The King's College of Our Lady and Saint Nicholas in Cambridge') was founded by the English King Henry VI (1421-1471) in 1441. It is the most famous and, many would argue, the most beautiful College in the world.

You can enter and leave the College through several gates. You will walk the paths and look at the various features we describe in various ways. Yet, to describe the features to you, we will imagine that you are standing outside the College, on King's Parade, in front of the front gate.

You will see to your right in the distance a white square building, the Senate House, designed by James Gibbs (1682-1754) and built in the early eighteenth century. In front of the Chapel is a giant chestnut tree, where King's meets the University, and in many ways symbolically the centre of the University and City. Adjacent to it you will see the famous Chapel of King's College.

In front of you is a long stone screen, built in the 1820s by William Wilkins in a revived medieval style (neo-Gothic). In the centre is the entrance, with the Porters' Lodge, the porters being in charge of many things in the College. In front of it there are cobbles. Under them are foundations of the brick building of 1693, uncovered when the cobbles were relayed in 1962, and, before that, medieval gardens. On the cobbles is a rare hexagonal Victorian pillar postbox, which was erected in front of King's in 1956, but was originally made between 1866 and 1879 and designed by John Wornham Penfold (1828-1909) and is hence known as a 'Penfold'.

If you walk down about fifty yards to your left, you will see several things. There is a blue plaque to the memory of the mathematician and computer scientist Alan Turing, about whom you will find out more when you stand on the bridge in King's. The computer revolution which Turing initiated was continued in various ways in the College. For example, beyond the Eagle pub in Bene't Street is the entry to number 4A Market Hill, where, in January 1979, Hermann Hauser and Chris Curry founded Acorn Computers. Hauser is an alumnus and Honorary Fellow of King's. Later the firm developed the Acorn RISC Machine technology (ARM) which is in almost every mobile device in the world. Hauser is also one of the leading figures in the development of 'The Cambridge Phenomenon', associated with the largest science park in Europe.

There is another plaque nearby celebrating the site of the White Horse Inn. According to legend, a group of English Protestant reformers met to discuss Lutheran ideas here from 1521. Among those who were said to meet were Thomas Cranmer (1489-1556), Hugh Latimer (c. 1485-1555) and Nicholas Ridley (c. 1502-1555), all of whom were later burnt as heretics at Oxford. Opposite King's in St Edward's Church in 1525 one of the group, Robert Barnes, gave what is believed to be the first openly reforming sermon in any English church, accusing the Catholic Church of heresy. It is known as the 'Cradle of the English Reformation'.

Near the plaques is a relatively recent statue of King Henry VIII (1491-1547), donated in the late nineteenth century. Henry inaugurated the Protestant Reformation in England and oversaw the completion of the Chapel, including the marvellous windows and the wooden screen on which are carved the initials of Henry and his then wife Anne Boleyn (c. 1500-1536).

Near the plaques are rooms where various well-known people associated with the College lived. One of these was the Professor of Fine Art and painter, Roger Fry (1866-1934), in room J10. Fry was one of the major figures in the growing appreciation of Impressionist and Chinese Art in Britain, a founding member of the artistic and literary circle known as the Bloomsbury Group, and one of the major patrons and friends of the Chinese poet Xu Zhimo (1897-1931).

Another with a Chinese connection was Arthur Waley (1889-1966) in J6. Waley translated many of the great classic novels and poems of Japan and China. He was a student and then Honorary Fellow of the College and mentor of the Chinese writer Xiao Qian (or Hsiao Ch'ien, 1910-1999).

Where the building ends, there is a narrow lane (King's Lane) which used to be the site of rooms for members of the College, known as 'The Drain'. Here, among others, lived Sri Aurobindo, formerly Ghose (1872-1950), the Indian mystic, academic, philosopher, writer, critic and political activist (arrested twice by the British). He lived in room M2 when he was in College in 1890. Aurobindo is now remembered in a special tree, planted in his memory in the Fellows' Garden in1997 by Sri Chinmoy.

Another resident in the Drain (N3 as an undergraduate), was John Maynard Keynes (1883-1946), economist and polymath, author of many books, and, among other things one of the architects of the post Second World War economic order at Bretton Woods. Keynes founded the Arts Theatre in Cambridge, was an important collector of early printed books and paintings (which he donated to the College), and the most munificent donor to the College since the Founder. Keynes' rooms when a Fellow were P3 (over the south gate) and after he married the Russian ballerina Lydia Lopokova (1892-1981), Flat 17(a) St Edward's Passage across from King's.

Keynes' influence helped to make the College famous for its economists. They included Sir Richard Stone (1913-1991) who in 1984 won the Nobel prize for developing an accounting model for national and international trading. Others at King's included the two senior advisors to the British and other governments, Lord Richard Kahn (1905-1989), who collaborated closely with Keynes, and Lord Nicholas Kaldor (1908-1986).

Turning around and walking down Bene't Street for about 30 yards, you will find another plaque at the entrance to the Eagle pub. This celebrates the discovery of the structure of DNA in 1953. Although neither Francis Crick (1916-2004) nor James Watson were at King's, they spent a great deal of time here - one of the most famous photographs of the pair shows them walking down a path in front of the Chapel, and Watson wrote his book *The Double Helix* in a room overlooking the back lawn of King's.

King's College Fellows played their parts in this revolution in physical biochemistry. Fred Sanger (1918-2013) in 1958 won a Nobel prize for sequencing insulin, and then a second one in 1980 for techniques used in sequencing nucleic acids. He is only the third person to have won two Nobel prizes in science. The Sanger Centre outside Cambridge is named after him. Another King's Fellow, Sydney Brenner, won a Nobel prize in 2002 for discoveries concerning genetic regulation of organ development and programmed cell death.

If you walk a little further and look to your right you will see Free School Lane, down which is the Old Cavendish Laboratory. This is where the double-helix structure of DNA was first discovered, where the electron and neutron were discovered, and where the atom was first split. King's produced other Nobel Prize winners who worked in or near here: in 1922 A.V. Hill (1886-1977) won a Nobel prize for his work relating to the production of heat in the muscle, and in 1948, Patrick Blackett (1897-1974) won another Nobel Prize working in the Old Cavendish.

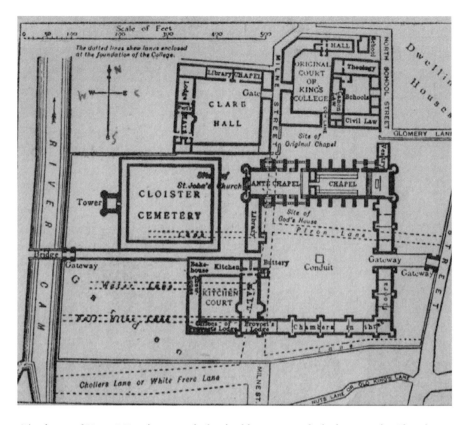

The design of Henry VI is shown in darker buildings, none of which except the Chapel were built during his life time

Front Lawn

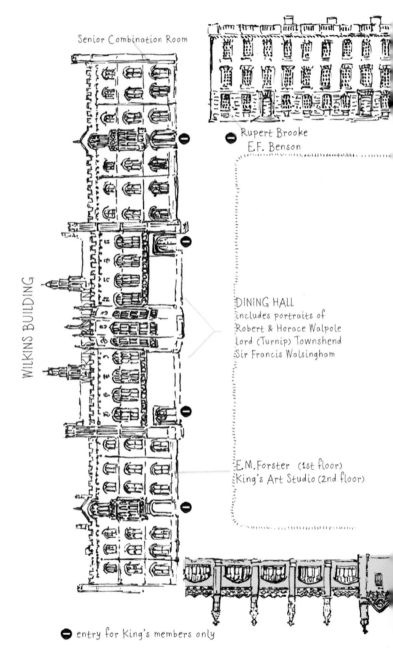

Senior Combination Room

WILKINS BUILDING

Rupert Brooke
E.F. Benson

DINING HALL
includes portraits of
Robert & Horace Walpole
lord (Turnip) Townshend
Sir Francis Walsingham

E.M. Forster (1st floor)
King's Art Studio (2nd floor)

⊖ entry for King's members only

Front lawn - please do not walk on the grass
Fountain and statue of the founder - Henry VI
Gibbs building, designed by James Gibbs and built in 1724
Gibbs arch ('Jumbo arch')
Rupert Brooke - romantic poet, 'The Old Vicarage Grantchester' etc
E.F. Benson - novelist, author of Mapp and Lucia and ghost stories

GIBBS

G.L. Dickinson
Charles Simeon

Wittgenstein's poker ⊖

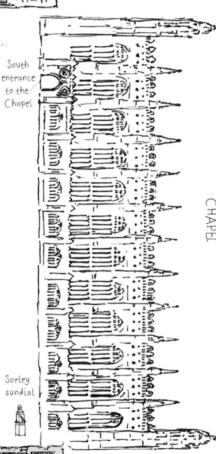

South entrance to the Chapel

Henry VI (founder's) Fountain

CHAPEL

Sorley sundial

Charles Simeon - influential evangelical clergyman, Simeon Trust founder
G.L. Dickinson - patron of Xu Zhimo, lover of China
Wittgenstein's Poker - meeting including Bertrand Russell, Wittgenstein and Popper
Sorley Sundial - from Scottish 17th church in memory of King's Professor
E.M. Forster - novelist, author of 'Passage to India', 'Howard's End' etc.
Dining Hall - with portraits of Robert and Horace Walpole, Lord Townshend etc.

Once you enter the front gate you will see a large lawn in front of you. This used to be crisscrossed with paths and even had trees on it. Now it is carefully preserved and only Fellows (Senior members of the College) and their guests can walk across it. This is partly to preserve it from being trampled to mud, partly as an exclusive right since the College is, in fact, a private space which is run as a Charitable Trust by the Fellows. To walk across it would be like going into a private house and wandering about the garden. Even walking on the paths is by special permission, and once a year the College is completely closed which prevents a 'right of way' becoming established. Remember that you are entering a private space, just as if you were going into someone's house.

In the centre of the lawn is a fountain with a statue of the founder of the College, King Henry VI. The fountain was built only in 1879 (though Henry VI intended there to be a conduit there). Much has happened around the fountain, including the notorious ducking of a student, the incident becoming incorporated into the mainly Oxford book *Brideshead Revisited* by Evelyn Waugh.

If you look straight ahead beyond the fountain you will see the long white building, built in 1724 by James Gibbs (hence known as the Gibbs Building). It is a good representative of the neo-classical style of the eighteenth century in England. At its centre is an arch, known to be large enough for an elephant to go through. Hence the building is also known as 'The Jumbo (elephant) House', and, among other things, a camel went through this arch on a charity fundraiser in 1999.

This is the building where the Fellows have lived and taught since it was built. Almost every window could tell a story. Starting at the bottom left (E1), this was occupied for a while by Rupert Brooke (1887-1915), scholar and Fellow. Brooke was a romantic poet and author, most famously, of 'The Old Vicarage, Grantchester' with its evocation of the Cambridge countryside. Earlier in this room was the writer E.F. Benson (1867-1940), son of an Archbishop of Canterbury and prolific writer, best known for his series of *Mapp and Lucia* novels. He was also an important ghost story writer and insightful describer of King's in his *As We Were: a Victorian Peepshow* and *David of King's*.

View from Rupert Brooke's rooms in Gibbs

Over the arch is a semi-circular window. The room behind this window was occupied by several distinguished figures. One was Charles Simeon (1759-1836) who is also remembered in the simple 'C.S.' on the floor of the Chapel half-way between the North and South doors. Simeon paid most of the cost of the bridge which now crosses the Cam and the walkway beyond that. Simeon was Fellow, Bursar, Dean and Vice Provost, and he is remembered as a Christian evangelical, inspiration for missionaries, and co-founder of the Church Missionary Society. He founded the Simeon Trust, and now Simeon Churches are spread over the country and the trustees have interests in nearly 200 parishes in over 40 dioceses.

Another who later lived in these same rooms was Goldsworthy Lowes Dickinson (1862-1932), author of many books including *Letters from John Chinaman* (1900). Dickinson was a pacifist, inventor of the term 'The League of Nations' and one of the founding committee of the League's precursor, the Bryce Group. He was the major patron and friend of Xu Zhimo in the College, and his close friend E.M. Forster (with whom he travelled to India), wrote his biography. There is a fountain-turned-flowerpot now in Chetwynd Court, a memorial to him, originally in Webb's court.

View from the corridor into the Dining Hall with portraits of the Walpoles

At the other end, in room H3, the Cambridge philosophical society met for many years. The one occasion when Bertrand Russell, Ludwig Wittgenstein and Karl Popper met there for a meeting led to a dispute. The account of what happened has given rise to a book, *Wittgenstein's Poker* by David Edmonds & John Eidinow. The poker is still held in the College.

Higher up the same staircase, Patrick Blackett lived in room H6 as a Fellow. He was an experimental physicist known for his work on cloud chambers, cosmic rays and paleomagnetism, winning the Nobel Prize for Physics in 1948. He also made a major contribution in World War II advising on military methodology and developing operational research.

As you look to the right, the medieval Chapel dominates the Front Court. It will be described separately, but two small things to look out for can be mentioned. One is the Sorley sundial, located in the corner near the front screen. This is named after the philosopher William Sorley, Fellow of King's in 1901. His ashes are buried in the Chapel and his wife gave the sundial to the College. It originally came from the old church of St Ann at Dunbar in East Lothian, Scotland.

At the other end of the south face of the Chapel, a few metres up the wall, you will see some spikes. These were placed to deter climbers, the famous 'Night Climbers of Cambridge', who used this particular corner to scale the Chapel.

If you look to the left you will see a row of buildings, built in mock medieval style in 1828 by Wilkins. The first staircase leads into the students' bar, lecture rooms, and also up A staircase to the rooms which are now the graduate students' rooms, but used to be those where E.M. Forster (1879-1970) lived in his last years. He was a student and Honorary Fellow (from 1945 on), novelist (*A Passage to India*, *Howard's End* and others), essayist and member of the Bloomsbury Group.

Beyond that, the large windows are those of the dining hall, again in neo-Gothic style by Wilkins, and reminding some of those who participate in the large dinners held there of scenes in J.K. Rowling's Hogwarts school dining hall. It can also strike visitors, especially Chinese, as a kind of 'Ancestor Hall', with portraits of many of the distinguished people who have passed through the College on the walls.

Among these are two members of the Walpole family. Sir Robert Walpole (1676-1745) was the first *de facto* British Prime Minister and holds the record as the longest serving British prime minister in history (1721-1742). His son Horace Walpole (1717-1797), was an art historian, literary figure, antiquarian and owner of Strawberry Hill House.

Also, there is a large portrait of Viscount Charles Townshend (1674-1738), brother-in-law of Sir Robert Walpole and a statesman. He is now best known as 'Turnip' Townshend, whose introduction of turnips for improving soil and for winter feeding on his large Norfolk estates was one of the key elements of the British agricultural revolution of the eighteenth century.

One portrait which is strangely missing in the College, is that of one of its most influential and interesting alumni, Sir John Harrington (or Harington) (c. 1560-1612). Harrington was a prominent courtier under Queen Elizabeth (he was Elizabeth's godson). He was a scholar, translating Ariosto's *Orlando Furioso* (he was banished from court until he finished his racy translation) and later fell into disfavour again for a satire. He installed the first of a new kind of flushing toilet called an Ajax in his manor at Kelston and wrote a book about it. This makes him one of the most influential figures in history, the father of the water closet (or W.C.)

View from Charles Simeon's rooms above Jumbo arch, Gibbs

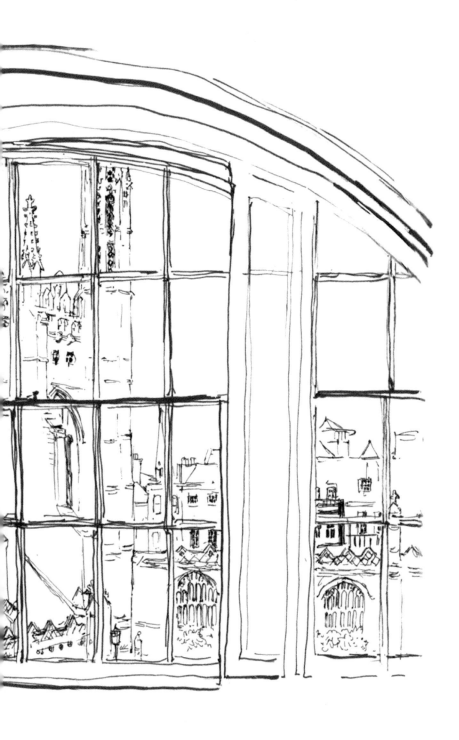

Back Lawn

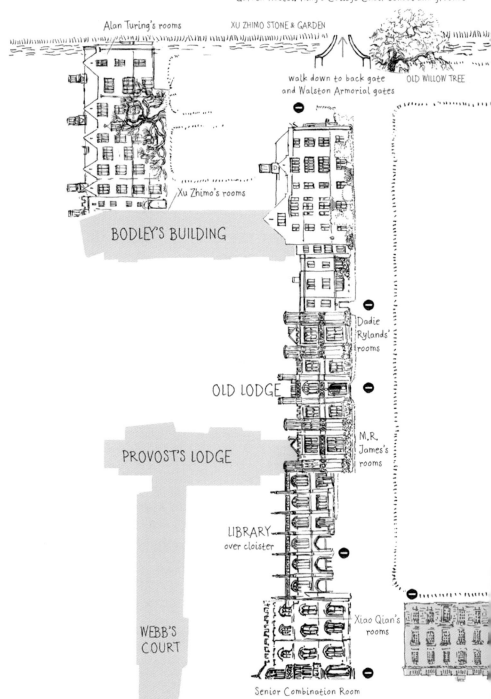

Alan Turing's rooms

to Fellows Garden (preserved Victorian garden)
Garden Hostel, King's College Choir School and grounds

XU ZHIMO STONE & GARDEN

walk down to back gate
and Walston Armorial gates

OLD WILLOW TREE

Xu Zhimo's rooms

BODLEY'S BUILDING

Dadie
'Rylands'
rooms

OLD LODGE

M.R.
James's
rooms

PROVOST'S LODGE

LIBRARY
over cloister

WEBB'S
COURT

Xiao Qian's
rooms

Senior Combination Room

SCHOLAR'S PIECE
field beyond river with mounds, cows
and famous view of the College from the Backs

RIVER CAM

Back Lawn - over parts of medieval Cambridge. Please do not walk on the grass

Senior Combination Room - where Fellows meet after dinner etc.

Xiao Qian - room of distinguished Chinese writer and friend of E.M. Forster

College Library - home to over one hundred thousand books and Archives Centre

Old Lodge - home to various Provosts, including ghost story writer M.R. James

Dadie Rylands - influential Shakespeare scholar linked to the Bloomsbury group

Clare College - second oldest Cambridge College: these buildings of 1638

Alan Turing - rooms where he wrote his first specification of computers & A.I.

Xu Zhimo - willow, stone and garden

CLARE COLLEGE

memorial stone to
Dadie Rylands

GIBBS

KING'S COLLEGE
CHAPEL

If you now go through the gap between the Wilkins Building and Gibbs, you will pass the Senior Combination Room where the Fellows meet, especially when they 'combine' for dinner and for formal meetings. Just above the Combination Room, in room D2, lived Xiao Qian, journalist, writer and translator who spent 1942-44 studying with E.M. Forster and 'Dadie' Rylands, about whom more below.

View onto Chapel from a window in the Senior Combination Room

Above the cloister on your left is the College Library, also built by Wilkins in 1828. This is used by students and staff and has a fine collection of over one hundred thousand books.

Student working in a corner of King's College Library

Through the pillars you will catch a glimpse of Webb's court, the south side of which is Webb's building where Keynes lived in P3, and above the south gate of which are the initials MRJ, MRJ being Montague Rhodes James.

Library on left and Old Provost's Lodge on right

James (1862-1936) was Provost or head of the College between 1905 and 1918, living in the Old Provost's Lodge, the next building beyond the arches/ library. In 1894 he wrote and published his first ghost story, and it became a custom to invite other Fellows and friends in to listen to a ghost story each Christmas. These annual stories were turned into several books, including *Ghost Stories of an Antiquary* (1904), establishing James as one of the world's greatest ghost story writers. He was also an extraordinary medieval scholar and Director of the Fitzwilliam Museum, Vice-Chancellor of Cambridge and later Provost of Eton, the only person in history to be head of both King's and Eton.

When the new Provost's Lodge was built behind the old one in 1927, some of the upper rooms in the Old Lodge were turned into Fellows' rooms. Among those who lived there was George 'Dadie' Rylands (1902-1999), one of the last members of the Bloomsbury Group, literary critic and central figure in the development of drama in Cambridge through the Marlowe Society. In his dining room in the Old Lodge looking out over the back lawn, Virginia Woolf set a dinner party in her novel *A Room of One's Own*. There is a stone inscribed in Latin to Rylands' memory on the ground at the west end of the Gibbs arch.

If you look to your right after arriving in the Back Court, you will also see the side of the neighbouring College, Clare. This is the second oldest College in Cambridge, founded in 1326, though the Old Court which overlooks King's lawn was built during the period 1638-1715.

Perhaps the most extraordinary thing you see is an absence – of buildings in a huge expanse of grass. This is the Back Lawn, probably the most photo-graphed academic lawn in the world. Until the purchase of the land by Henry VI in the 1440s, the main street of Cambridge ran through where the Chapel would be built - in the line from the small street which leads to the north gate, then continued in what is now Queens' Lane. The busy area of gardens, streets, a church and a small port for boats was all cleared away at the King's decree, leaving only some of the houses along what is now King's Parade.

The foundations of the pre-1440s world are buried, but when the weather has been dry for some weeks, it is possible to see the shapes of old buildings and paths through the grass, a suitably ghostly presence for the ghost-writing Provost James to have looked out on. Because no subsequent building has been done, this is arguably the most important potential site for medieval town archaeology in England.

As you look out across the lawn you may see the strange sight of long poles moving along beyond the lawn. When you walk on, these will be revealed to be punt poles, which are used to push long flat boats on the River Cam. Commercial punting is relatively recent, dating from the early twentieth century and introduced from the River Thames, although the pushing of flat boats with poles along the Cam dates back to an earlier period. For many centuries, the main boats on the river were barges, busiest until the wiping away of the port in the 1440s, but continuing until they were replaced by the railways in the middle of the nineteenth century. At first these barges were pulled by horses walking along the banks, but when the Colleges took over the sides, a stone walkway was built at the bottom of the river and the horses waded along, as in this early engraving.

A plate engraved by W & J. Walker and published in 1793
The barges being drawn up the river by horse can be seen, and the punting of pleasure boats also

The river is an invisible boundary between the manicured lawn and the rougher parkland beyond. It is like the traditional barrier made in many English country estates and called a 'ha ha' (a recessed vertical barrier, which is invisible and allows the illusion that there is no barrier at all). Here you will also catch your first glance, to the left, of one of the most famous trees in the world, the willow celebrated in a Chinese poem which will be described shortly.

Beyond the punt-poles the open ground continues. This field is known as 'Scholar's Piece', because the scholarly King's Fellows and students were allowed to keep their horses there. To encourage the impression that this is the rougher parkland of an English estate, there are trees, wild flowers, long grass and, in the summer, a number of cows. There are now beehives, where bees are to pollinate the College orchard and Fellows' Garden. There are remains of what used to be an island with a dovecote, then an ice house. The mounds in the field were created by digging the ditches surrounding the island.

From the University Almanack of 1802. The old position of the King's Bridge, in line with the arch through the Gibbs building, can be seen on the right under the trees

If you walk down the left-hand side of the lawn you will reach King's Bridge. From this bridge you can look up at the room (X17) where Alan Turing (1912-1954), as a young Fellow of 23, wrote a paper in early 1936 in which he outlined, for the first time, how an electronic computer could be made and Artificial Intelligence could be developed. Later, as a code breaker at

Bletchley Park, his work in deciphering the German secret codes (recounted in the film *The Imitation Game*) helped England win the second world war.

If you walk on from the bridge, alongside the wild flowers, you will reach the back gate. The gate-posts date from 1818-20, when the bridge was built. The iron gate itself, including the shield, was installed in 1924, donated by Sir Charles Walston (1856-1927), Fellow of the College from 1894 and Director of the Fitzwilliam Museum.

If you go out of this gate, and look back, you will experience the most famous view of the College. The walk along the bank of a little tributary affords a good view of what is known as 'The Backs'. The part owned by King's extends from the wide strip starting on King's Parade, through the Front and Back courts, and across Scholar's Piece. Across the busy road the strip continues, turning into the Fellows' Garden, an unusually well preserved Victorian garden, open to staff and students, and on occasion (for example during the summer for Shakespeare plays) to the public. There are two student hostels and a fruit orchard and nuttery beyond the Fellows' Garden.

Crossing the busy street at the pedestrian light provides a small detour up West Road. Across from the Fellows' Garden is the 2006 Stephen Hawking building of Gonville & Caius College. Near here is the house where another distinguished Chinese visiting scholar at King's, Yeh Chun-chan (or Ye Junjian, 1914-1998) lived while he studied at King's at the end of the Second World War (1945-48). He went back to become one of the greatest translators of Western writing into Chinese, including the complete works of Hans Christian Andersen (for which he was knighted), as well as an autobiographical novel series starting with *The Mountain Village*.

Finally, beyond the hostels, are the grounds and buildings of the King's College Choir School. Here the choristers for the famous choir are taught. If you are lucky you may see the little choristers with their Etonian top hats and short gowns processing through the grounds to the Chapel.

The people mentioned in this guide are almost all dead. It is invidious to choose between living King's persons, and indeed there are so many interesting and influential ones. It is worth making a partial exception, however, in the case of King's women, since women became students of the College only from 1972 and consequently would be only recently represented. Thus, it is worth noting among many notable such women, Dame Judith Weir (composer and Master of the Queen's music), Zadie Smith (novelist) and Lily Cole (model and actress).

The Chapel

James Malton, 1794, the East end of the Chapel, with the Old Provost's Lodge and buildings along King's Parade in front of the College, and the Senate House on the right

MANY BOOKS HAVE been written about the Chapel, so we do not intend to add to them. Here are five things worth noting. The first is the most amazing fan-vaulted ceiling, an exquisite soaring experience described in some of the poetry quoted later.

Knight, Charles (1845). Old England: A Pictorial Museum

The stone ceiling is brought down to the ground along fine thin columns, which somehow hold the enormous weight. It is difficult to understand why the Chapel does not collapse. Part of the secret lies in the massive flying buttresses hidden as walls of the side-chapels. Another part of the explanation is hidden in the area above the fan vaulting, between that roof and the outer roof. In a vast loft, there are several hundred huge ancient oak beams holding together the walls so that they are not thrust apart by the weight of the ceiling.

The second thing to note are the stained glass windows, telling the story of the Bible. They were made in the early sixteenth century and are one of the two finest sets of stained glass of that period.

VIEW BETWEEN THE ROOFS OF KING'S COLLEGE CHAPEL.

Thirdly, there is the wooden screen dividing the chancel, occupied during services by the priests and Choir, from the nave, occupied during services by the rest of the congregation. It is thought to be the finest example of a wooden screen of that era north of the Alps. It is continued in the beautiful carved wooden stalls for Fellows and Choir beyond the screen, as shown below.

Detail of Henry VIII and Anne Boleyn's initials...

...on the south side of the wooden screen dividing the Chapel

The fourth, if you are fortunate, is the Choir, which sings during the service each day during term at 5.30PM and in services on Sundays and special occasions such as the Carol services. The wonderful acoustic adds to the effect of what is often stated to be one of the two most beautiful male voice choirs in Europe.

Fifthly, splendidly set off by the architecture, is the painting of the 'Adoration of the Magi' by Rubens, placed behind the altar.

It is well to remember that the Chapel took many years to build, as the diagram below shows, even though the amazing ceiling was built in a mere three years.

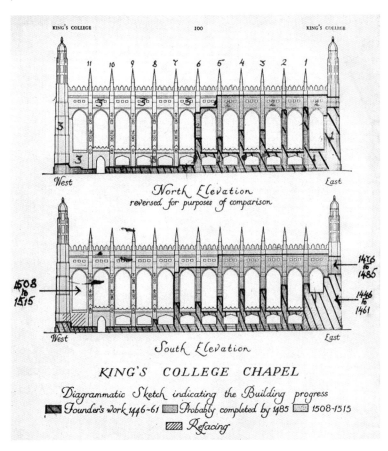

The Xu Zhimo willow, stone and garden

Memorial stone in memory of Xu Zhimo, placed by the bridge at King's in 2008

Xu Zhimo (1897-1931) was a young Chinese scholar who, at the invitation of Lowes Dickinson, came to be an associate member of King's College for eighteen months in 1921-22. He fell in love with the College and its grounds and with English romantic poetry and became one of China's best-known modern poets with his 'Second Farewell to Cambridge'. Yet, for the next eighty years, very few people in Cambridge knew that Xu had passed through the College. Then in 2008 a memorial stone of white Beijing marble, with the first and last lines of the poem engraved on it, was presented to the College and placed in the ground beside the King's bridge over the Cam.

In 2014 a photographic exhibition on Xu's life and works was held in the College Chapel, and a booklet on *Xu Zhimo, Cambridge and China* was published for the exhibition. From 2015 onwards an international poetry and arts festival named after him has been held annually in the College. Then, in 2015, preparations began to be made for a Xu Zhimo Friendship Garden near the stone, based on Daoist and Buddhist symbolism and Chinese plants. A winding path between the Yin and the Yang has been made with the second and third lines of the poem in Chinese and English engraved on it. There is a 'crescent moon' bench in memory of the Crescent Moon Society which Xu set up when he returned to China, hoping to use it to bring Cambridge, Bloomsbury and England to China. The garden was launched in 2018 as the first Chinese garden in Cambridge.

The willow tree by the bridge celebrated in Xu Xhimo's poem must be one of the most famous trees in the world.

There is strong evidence from a pre-1899 photograph as well as the circumference of the trunk that Xu's willow is the one we see today. It is a tree Xu would have passed many times, especially when he lived in room

Bodley's court, with Xu Zhimo's room at top left, Alan Turing's room at top right

V7 at the top of the square tower in the corner in Bodley's court.

Xu Zhimo wrote his 'Second Farewell to Cambridge' in a shortened version in 1928, after his third visit to Cambridge. It is filled with longing for Cambridge, for his first love affair, and for England and its poetry.

Every Chinese schoolchild learns it by heart. Within three years of writing it, Xu was killed in a plane crash, his dreams of bringing Cambridge and Bloomsbury to China unfulfilled.

Second Farewell to Cambridge

Quietly, quietly, I am leaving
Just as quietly as I came.
Gently, I wave goodbye
To the clouds in the Western sky.

The golden willow on the bank of the Cam
Stands like a bride in the sunset.
Her reflection shimmers in the water,
And ripples in my heart.

The rushes in the soft river bed
Sway and glisten underwater.
I'd gladly be a river reed
Tossed by the currents of the Cam.

In the shadow of the elm is a pool
Not of clear spring water,
But a rainbow from heaven
Crushed and crumpled among the duckweed
Leaving only a rainbow-like dream.

Searching for a dream?

Take a long pole and punt
Gently back towards the greenest of green grass
In a boat brimful of starlight,
Singing out loud in the splendour of the starlight

I cannot sing aloud now.
The flute and pan-pipes of parting have gone silent.
Even the clamorous summer insects are hushed for me.
Silence tonight in Cambridge.

Quietly, quietly I am leaving
Just as quietly as I came.
Careful not to brush away with my sleeve
The faintest wisp of a cloud.

(Translated by Yao Liang 梁维耀, Choo Liang 梁莲珠 and MickLe Moignan)

Peculiar Institutions

DESCRIBING THE PEOPLE and buildings of the College only leads us on to deeper questions. How was King's made, how was it preserved, why is it the only such place in the world? Here we move to another level, that of institutional structures, to law, politics and economics through history. I will single out three things. The first two King's shares with the other older Colleges of Cambridge. The third is the set of defining features linked to the original founding of the College.

King's as a religious foundation

The presence of the grand Chapel is a reminder that in order to understand the older Oxford and Cambridge Colleges you have constantly to remember that they derive from the pattern of medieval monasteries. The Colleges were often religious foundations, set up to pray for their founder, as well as to educate young men.

This explains why, like monks, Fellows were not allowed to marry in King's and other Colleges until the 1860s. It also explains why most Kingsmen had to be members of the Church of England until the same period, and why all students had to prove that they were members of the Church. Fellows and students had to attend services every day during term time during those centuries, and theology was a major subject in the syllabus.

So, until about one hundred and fifty years ago, when the rules were dramatically changed, the nearest analogy is to a Christian or Buddhist monastery. Even today, the Fellows have to take an oath to uphold the College as a place of religion, as well as education, learning and research. There is still, with the bells and services and a 'Provost' as the head, a feeling of a religious foundation, and the Dean or head of the Chapel is equivalent to a Bishop.

How do the Colleges and the University overlap?

One of the most puzzling features of Oxford and Cambridge for visitors is how the University and Colleges are linked to each other. Basically, the

Colleges are like a person's home, and the University like the wider world. Students often leave home for the first time for a long period when they go to university, unless they are among the tiny proportion who have been away to a boarding school.

Undergraduate students are accepted by the College and the Colleges are the place where they live, eat, work and pray (if they are so minded). Their studies are organised and often implemented through the College. Yet they go out into the University for lectures, libraries, seminars and, if they are scientists, laboratories.

Since both Oxford and Cambridge for a number of centuries took undergraduate students at a much younger age, often from fourteen or fifteen, it was even more evident then that the Colleges acted as a kind of foster home for young people, similar to the role of apprentice masters. The Colleges provided, and still do, intellectual apprenticeships, at the end of which a person is an adult with a trade or craft – a Master of Arts (M.A.).

So, in Cambridge, there are two distinct bodies. There is the University, encompassing, but separate from, all the Colleges. It is in charge of the other institutions like the University Library, Faculties and Departments, museums and laboratories. And there are the Colleges, which are autonomous and with a strong separate identity.

One advantage of this somewhat complex double structure of powerful Colleges and powerful University, is that it tends to prevent the concentration of too much power in one institution. A Professor in the University, or a Fellow in a College, cannot crush or subdue his or her juniors, staff or students, as often happens in universities without such a College system.

The Colleges are not subject-based, the undergraduates and teachers pursuing a very wide range of disciplines, unlike Departments and Faculties. One or two may have a special reputation for a subject, Trinity Hall for law, Trinity for science, King's for music, but, on the whole, there is no specialisation. So, students and teachers spend their time (away from the formal teaching) with people in many different disciplines and are forced outwards.

Humans seem to thrive in small, face-to-face, groups like early bands of Hunter Gatherers. They enjoy being in a place where they know many, if not all, of the people they meet and have known them for more than a short while and in many different contexts. Colleges give people a sense of 'we-ness', of the warmth (and sometimes confrontation) of inclusion and longer-term relationships. As Cambridge expanded over the last centuries, the University did this by adding medium-sized units, more Colleges of a few hundred students and Fellows, rather than making mega-Colleges. The intimacy was preserved.

What is unusual about King's?

What sets King's apart from all other Oxford and Cambridge Colleges is its point of origin, the way it was set up in the 1440s by King Henry VI as a royal foundation. Henry went to a great deal of trouble to create strong protective safeguards for his proposed College and its independence. He obtained a number of Papal Bulls (proclamations by the Pope) to secure the College independence from the power of the Archbishop of Canterbury and the nearest bishopric at Ely. The College was to have its own 'peculiar' ecclesiastical jurisdiction, for example in the proving or administration of wills and trying of certain offences.

Likewise, the King did not want the College to be under the governance of the University of Cambridge, so it was created independent of the Chancellor of the University and through many centuries this was interpreted to mean that the College could award its own degrees. King's students until the later nineteenth century did not need to take University examinations to proceed to their Master's degree. The College had its own academical jurisdiction.

Thirdly, the Founder had simultaneously set up the royal foundation of Eton College, a public school near Windsor. He thought it would be good to link Eton and King's, as in 1382 Winchester and New College Oxford had been tied. So for some four hundred years all Scholars at King's had come from Eton College.

Finally, after a first modest plan of 1441, Henry decided to build a much grander College, in particular from 1446 and the start of the huge Chapel. Though Henry died before he could complete this, his successors Henry VII and Henry VIII completed the Chapel. Henry VI endowed the College with a large area in central Cambridge on which he planned to build his new College, but in fact it was only from the eighteenth century that these grounds began to be seriously developed.

These provisions lie behind the very special history of the College. It is set apart, has a special atmosphere, in particular with a tradition of being involved in many subjects outside the strictly academic, including music, drama and literature. And its magnificent buildings are not hemmed in by other buildings as are the other great Colleges such as Trinity, Cambridge and Christ Church, Oxford.

By chance this early peculiarity was in large part preserved and King's now feels like a separate stately home placed in the middle of a busy city. With its royal coat of arms and seal, royal colours of purple, and Statutes which have to be approved by the King or Queen in Council, and hence are very difficult to change, it is different from any other College in either Oxford or Cambridge.

The cost of these peculiarities has to be borne in mind. The exclusion of all but old Etonians for nearly two thirds of its history led, at times, to stagnation. The great lawns at the front and back were achieved only at the cost of much destruction, as the plan on the end-papers shows. Only with the building of Gibbs on the cleared site in 1728 did the College begin to develop its extensive buildings. Before that the College was still located in what are now the Old Schools to the north of the Chapel, where the original gate of the College still survives.

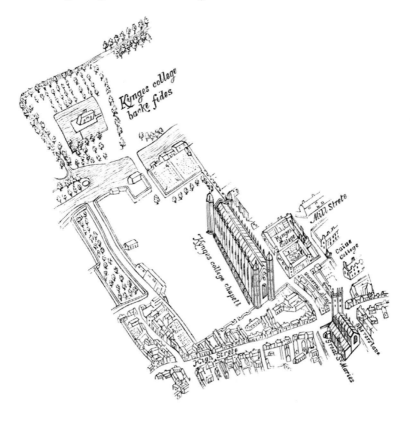

Old Court, the original location of King's College, now part of the Old Schools or University administration, taken from Cooper, Memorials 1866

Magical landscapes

River

You MAY THINK that it is just a coincidence that the two great medieval English universities, Oxford and Cambridge, are threaded by rivers and incorporate a ford and a bridge into their names.

Yet this connection with water is part of the secret of their special nature. Willows by water, boats on water, clouds in the water, buildings reflected over the water, bridges curving over water are among the most enduring images of King's.

Chinese visitors say that the watery landscape of Cambridge and the Fens is what attracts them most, perhaps evoking the famous Chinese landscapes of the mountains and rivers and water margins of China, the mighty Yangtze, the mists of Guillin or the canal cities of the eastern seaboard. The River Cam does many things for King's, even after it ceased to be a great thoroughfare for traffic from all over England in the nineteenth century.

The presence of water gives life to the buildings because the river is constantly moving, both with its internal force and as a mirror of the skies and winds. It also adds to the sense that King's is an ancient stately home, like Blenheim or Stowe, where lakes and rivers are used by the architects to give a sense of that ordered wildness which the English love. It is nature tamed and domesticated, yet nature still.

Beauty lies in balance and contrast. To have a green space where cows graze the rough turf and swans swim on one side and the smoothest of lawns and mighty buildings on the other creates a special delight.

Architecture

In *The Stones of Venice*, John Ruskin draws attention to the irregularity and spontaneity of English art. He contrasts continental, Baroque, art with its formal gardens, central plaza, heavy classical-style buildings and straight streets – authoritarian, planned, dominating – with the crooked, asymmetrical, unbalanced, art of the Gothic north.

King's is a fine example of what Ruskin was talking about. It is illustrated in poetry, for instance in the famous line by the King's poet Rupert Brooke when he compares the German flower beds where everything is in neat lines to the 'English unofficial rose' which grows as it will.

The crookedness is shown in the jumbled nature of King's, styles from different centuries thrown together. The Gothic tensions of sweeping contending forces reach their highest expression in King's College Chapel. It somehow feels unfinished, still soaring and aspiring, impossible in its distribution of forces in the huge weight apparently carried along its slender fan vaulting and columns.

The Chapel feels like a paper lantern floating in the Fens, especially when the light streams through the gleaming jewels of its stained glass. It is dream-like yet solid, its vertical lines lifting the whole city into the wide grey skies. It draws the eyes across the meadows and is balanced by the horizontal lines of Clare College and the Gibbs building.

As Virginia Woolf wrote in *Jacob's Room*,

They say the sky is the same everywhere… But above Cambridge – anyhow above the roof of King's College Chapel – there is a difference. Out at sea a great city will cast a brightness into the night. Is it fanciful to suppose the sky, washed into the crevices of King's College Chapel, lighter, thinner, more sparkling than the sky elsewhere? Does Cambridge burn not only into the night, but into the day?

The northern, irregular, energetic Gothic world that grew after the collapse of the Roman Empire is preserved in Cambridge as a constant reminder of something which stands apart from the constant tendency towards bureaucratic rationalisation, centralisation and the demand for homogeneity and standardisation.

The irregularity applies not just to the buildings, but to everything in Cambridge. The regulations of the University, the arrangement of the teaching system, the lay-out of the streets, the shape of the river, the cacophony of different arts, all are distinguished by variety, asymmetry, a jumble of bits tacked onto other dissimilar bits. The only synthesis is provided by the resolution of opposing forces.

Inside this Gothic world, darting here and there, live and work the students, staff and Fellows. They have been allowed to develop strong, often idiosyncratic and distinctive minds and manners. They are not subjected to a central censorial bureau. They are not forced to conform too closely to normal codes of manners.

We are in a world well described by Lewis Carroll in *Alice's Adventures in Wonderland*; there is the odd Mad Hatter, game of croquet on the croquet lawn in the Fellows' Garden, strange tea party, many a Cheshire (or Schrödinger's) cat in the bizarre theories put forward. King's is a maze of ingenuity, experiment and game playing. It looks so serene and calm on the surface, yet beneath its quiet dignity there is a constantly seething, provisional, unbalanced, but fruitful exploration of the world amidst its ever-changing, irregular buildings and spaces.

So King's remains a fairy College, verging on something out of a Charles Dickens story. Yet alongside the revived Gothic of much of the nineteenth-century creations, there really is a medieval College surviving in part. There are medieval laws and the strange irregularities of a medieval, feudal, Christian civilisation preserved in many of its customs and ideas. It is ultra-modern in certain aspects, apparently rejecting modernity in others. It is a strange ensemble that seems doomed to comic failure yet somehow works and delights.

Chapel

The Chapel is a symbol of King's and Cambridge. Each of its thin pillars can be seen as one branch of the academic traditions – history, mathematics, philosophy, physics and others. The pillars soar upwards and then join with others in the amazing fanned roof where all the human efforts to understand our world feed into each other and come to rest, like a shower that never falls. It is a seamless and perfect resolution of disparate pressures. Like much of Cambridge, the Chapel is very old, yet it also feels as if it is young, fresh, clean and vigorous.

Between these threads of stone are the equally extraordinary windows, based on the great art of the Renaissance, and filled with deep colour.

John Milton
But let my due feet never fail
To walk the studious Cloysters pale,
And love the high embowèd Roof,
With antick Pillars massy proof,
And storied Windows richly dight,
Casting a dimm religious light.

William Wordsworth
But, from the arms of silence – list! O list!
The music bursteth into second life; –
The notes luxuriate – every stone is kissed
By sound, or ghost of sound, in mazy strife;
Hearth-thrilling strains, that cast before the eye
Of the Devout, a veil of ecstasy!

John Betjeman
File into yellow candlelight, fair choristers of King's
Lost in shadowy silence of canopied Renaissance stalls:
In blazing glass above the dark glow skies and thrones and wings
Blue, ruby, gold and green between the whiteness of the walls
And with what rich precision the stonework soars and springs
To fountain out a spreading vault - a shower that never falls.

This theme of being transported into another more ethereal realm, a parallel world with its echoes of Paradise, runs through many of the other descriptions of the Chapel. The novelist Henry James wrote in his travel memoir 'English Hours':

It is a Cathedral without aisles or columns or transepts, but (as a compensation) with such a beautiful slimness of clustered tracery soaring along the walls and spreading, bending and commingling in the roof, that its simplicity seems only a richness the more. I stood there for a quarter of an hour on a Sunday morning; there was no service, but in the choir behind the great screen which divides the chapel in half the young choristers were rehearsing for the afternoon. The beautiful boy-voices rose together and touched the splendid vault; they hung there, expanding and resounding, and then, like a rocket that spends itself, they faded and melted toward the end of the building. It was positively a choir of angels.

Even for non-believers the Chapel feels miraculous, a time and a space for transporting the spirit into other worlds. When the colours and shapes are added to the ethereal voices, drifting and echoing in the ways the poets describe, one almost feels as if the angels on the organ have come to life.

The Chapel touches all who visit it. Think of Newton walking through it while he was doing his experiments on light and the way in which glass could be used to break it into its separate colours. As Thomas Hardy wrote, 'Wordsworth's ghost, too, seemed to haunt the place, lingering and wandering on somewhere alone in the fan-traceried vaulting.' Charles Darwin wrote of his time in Cambridge that 'I acquired a strong taste for music, and used very often to time my walks so as to hear on week days the anthem in King's College Chapel. This gave me intense pleasure, so that my backbone would sometimes shiver.'

Colours

The special colour of King's, on its scarfs, and other symbols, is purple. Purple is traditionally the royal colour in England, and as a royal College, King's is entitled to this colour. The predominant colours of the place itself are almost not colours at all. They are the mellow brown of sun-warmed walls, the greys and whites of all varieties of stone from Wales, from Yorkshire and from France. They are the black of gowns and cold nights. It is a sepia landscape, like an old photograph.

Yet, against this Chinese ink-wash background there are sudden vivid splashes. There is the vivid green of budding willows, the scarlet of academic gowns at feasts, the impossible blue of summer days over the soaring pinnacles of the Chapel. All come together in the incomparable miracle of the bended bubbles of light in the stained glass whose imperfections soak up and soften the glow of the sunlight in the splendour of King's College Chapel.

Colours, like surfaces and shapes, are used to give the eye variety through contrast. The Carol Service at King's is mainly black and white, with sudden golden candles and the scarlet of the Choir. The grey buildings are relieved by the lawns and flowers, the formal, tightly mowed grass is set off by trees which grow as they will in the semi-wild meadow of Scholar's Piece with its cows and buttercups.

Some of the colours are caught by the poet John Betjeman:

The white of windy Cambridge courts, the cobbles brown and dry,
The gold of plaster Gothic with ivy overgrown –
The apple-red, the silver fronts, the wide green flats and high,
The yellowing elm-trees circled out on islands of their own –
Oh, here behold all colours change that catch the flying sky
To waves of pearly light that heave along the shafted stone.

Across this stage, the colours of the entire world flow, saris and tartans, grave suits and shorts, faces from every continent and voices speaking many of the languages of the world. They drift like blown leaves through the old buildings and then are gone and the College settles back into its routines, apparently unchanged.

Heritage

The tension between an artificially preserved 'heritage' site, neat but dead on the one hand, or being swamped by change, is reasonably managed and is one of the attractions of King's. Visitors are aware that this is not just a museum, a mausoleum – a Stonehenge or Great Wall of China.

King's is a working educational institution with a strong, insistent, life of its own, dedicated to teaching and research and with many hundreds of students, staff and Fellows. Yet it is also a funnel into a more remote, medieval, world which is otherwise only observable rather accidentally in England.

King's is a vast performance, set on a grand stage, working out the themes of continuity and Englishness, of coping with the strains of simultaneously never being fully modern, while, in other ways, moving rapidly with the times. It is arguable that King's was a cradle of the modern world at the Reformation; but more recently it has been so again, in several disciplines including economics, computing and molecular biology. Yet King's also protects an older world of values and ideas.

Sounds

King's is filled with sound and silence. The music, the church bells, open-air madrigals on the river, rock bands at the King's Affair, recently the performance of the Chinese kun-cu opera, and above all the world famous College Choir are part of the enchantment. From the start, the fact that the College was based round religious services filled with plainchant and ancient music meant that College life was punctuated by music. The College Hall and particularly the Chapel provide a wonderful place for performances so that there has been a thread of music running through the five hundred years of King's history.

All of this is symbolised and brought to a climax each Christmas by the Carol Services from King's where the Choir in their scarlet and white robes send their voices up through the candle light into the dim vaults of the echoing ceiling.

It seems likely that music has seeped into the consciousness of most of those who have lived and worked in Cambridge, soothing or exciting, but always contributing to the way they think and feel. That the medieval carols, often with archaic words, but with harmonies and melodies which still touch our hearts, should have remained so constant, yet ever changing, is another example of that blend of past and present which is so distinctive about King's. Shakespeare's line 'Bare ruin'd choirs where late the sweet birds sang' reminds us that the music of the College is not just that created by great musicians and choirs, but that it is also full of bird song.

In between the music and the sound of bells and the wind, there are the moments of contrasted stillness. With traffic just about kept at bay, there is still silence in King's, of misty mornings with punts gliding down the Cam, of the sun breaking through the stained-glass windows in an empty Chapel. Cambridge is a casket of sounds, as it is of shapes and colours, preciously maintained over six centuries.

Further information

Books and articles:

E.F. Benson, *As We Were: A Victorian Peep-Show* (1930), chapter 7
M.R. James, *Eton and King's* (1926)
Rodney Tibbs, *King's College Chapel, Cambridge; The story and the renovation* (1970)
Patrick Wilkinson, *A Century of King's, 1873-1972* (1980)
Patrick Wilkinson, *Kingsmen of a Century, 1873-1972* (1980)
John Saltmarsh, 'King's College' in *A History of the County of Cambridge*, vol III ed. J.O.C. Roach, (1967), pp. 376-407
Francis Woodman, *The Architectural History of King's College Chapel* (1986)
Christopher Morris, *King's College, A Short History* (1989)
Josephine Warrior and Tim Rawle, *A Guide to King's College Chapel* (1994)
Noel Annan, *The Dons* (2000)
Karl Sabbagh, *A Book of King's* (2010)
Ross Harrison, *Our College Story* (2015)
Zilan Wang, *Xu Zhimo Cambridge and China* (2016)
Zeeman, N., and Massing, J.M., (eds), *King's College Chapel 1515-2015: Art, Music and Religion in Cambridge* (2015)

Web resources:

There are video interviews of 45 Fellows of Kings and alumni at:
https://www.sms.cam.ac.uk/collection/1092396
There are 88 films about King's and Cambridge, in the form of short interviews, at:
https://www.sms.cam.ac.uk/collection/1283730
King's College has an informative website, including a virtual tour, at:
http://www.kings.cam.ac.uk
King's shop has a website at:
https://shop.kings.cam.ac.uk
This includes links to various other books on King's and its Chapel

Acknowledgements

The engravings in the text are reproduced from materials in the King's College Archives, with kind permission of the Provost and Fellows of the College.

All the illustrations, apart from the engravings, including the front and back covers, were drawn by Bridget Strevens Marzo.

The photograph of the James Malton watercolour painting on pages 24-25 is the copyright of Adrian Boutel and Elizabeth Savage.

We would like to show our appreciation by thanking the following individuals who have made this publication possible:

Sponsors
Yanjin HE & Ke XIANG
Zihao Kimmey WANG & Ziqi WANG
Yisha XUE

Management Committee
Zilan WANG
Yanjin HE
Zihao Kimmey WANG

Management Team
James O'Sullivan   Yuchen QIN
Dalong GE   Xiaoya XUN
Li NING

Logistics Co-ordinators
Jinyu Tina ZHANG   William ZHAO
Wen Helen HE   Xilun JIANG
Anika ZHANG